COMMUNITY CONNECTIONS

KATIE'S KROPS
CHARITIES STARTED BY KIDS!
BY MELISSA SHERMAN PEARL

Published in the United States of America by Cherry Lake Publishing
Ann Arbor, Michigan
www.cherrylakepublishing.com

Reading Adviser: Marla Conn MS, Ed., Literacy specialist, Read-Ability, Inc.

Photo Credits: © Photo used with permission from Katie's Krops, cover, 7, 11, 13, 15, 17, 19, 21; © Rawpixel.com/Shutterstock Images, 5; © Monkey Business Images/ Shutterstock Images, 9

LIBRARY OF CONGRESS CATALOGING-IN-PUBLICATION DATA HAS BEEN FILED AND IS AVAILABLE AT CATALOG.LOC.GOV

Cherry Lake Publishing would like to acknowledge the work of The Partnership for 21st Century Learning. Please visit *www.p21.org* for more information.

Printed in the United States of America
Corporate Graphics

KATIE'S KROPS

CONTENTS

SOME INGREDIENTS ARE BIGGER THAN OTHERS

Food insecurity is defined by the United States Department of Agriculture as the occasional lack of access to enough food for the household. According to statistics, one out of every six people in America faces hunger.

Families with children are more at risk of hunger than families without children.

Katie Stagliano and her family have always been grateful for their life in South Carolina. Many dinner conversations focused on how lucky they were to enjoy a healthy meal together every night as many families went to bed hungry. In 2008, when Katie grew an amazing 40-pound (18-kilogram) cabbage from a **seedling** received in her third grade class, she knew it was something special.

Katie and her family were fortunate, but 17% of South Carolina's population lives in poverty.

THINK!

Katie firmly believes that it doesn't matter how small your actions are. They may still have a ripple effect and help other people. What's a small thing you can do to help change someone's life for the better?

7

SHARING IS CARING

Katie, age 9, started thinking about what she could do with this outstanding **bounty**. The cabbage was far too large for her and her family to eat. She decided to donate it to her local soup kitchen. The kitchen's director suggested she come back to help serve the meal.

Two days later, she returned and got to serve 275 guests. She couldn't believe that one not-so-little

Soup kitchens helped many people in America during the Great Depression.

cabbage helped feed so many. This experience changed her life. It inspired her to create Katie's Krops, a youth-run collection of gardens that donates their **harvests** to organizations that feed the hungry.

Before there was a nonprofit, though, there was Katie's next garden. She asked her parents if they could start a garden in their yard and continue helping the soup kitchen. They, of course, said yes.

Tomatoes are actually a fruit and not a vegetable.

Katie's 40-pound (18-kg) cabbage helped feed 275 people. If the average cabbage weighs about 2 pounds (1 kg), how many would you need to feed the same number of people?

11

Their encouragement inspired her to write a letter to her school explaining what she'd done with her cabbage as well as her goal. By fourth grade, her school gave her a plot of land the size of a football field to plant a garden.

The average American eats about 400 pounds (181 kg) of vegetables each year.

YOUR WISH (AND KROP) WILL BE GRANTED

Creating two gardens wasn't enough for this budding **philanthropist**. With support from her community as well as from kids across the country, she needed to do more. She **resolved** to offer **grants** to kids ages 9 to 16 so they could grow gardens in their own communities and donate the fresh produce. This would feed more

Growing a vegetable garden can take a lot of patience and practice.

LOOK!

Katie's Krops uses ladybugs to eat bugs that can harm the harvests. What other kinds of organic gardening practices can be used on gardens? Take a look online or at the library to find the answers.

people while **empowering** kids to help others.

To apply for a grant, kids create written proposals answering a number of questions. Where would they grow their garden? Who would help them with it? Where would their harvests be donated? Katie and her mom, Stacy, wanted to understand what the kids' gardens would be like and make sure there was a **maintenance** plan.

Once approved, the kids receive many helpful tools. Gift cards to local

Compost is made by recycling food- and yard-waste to make healthy soil that helps plants grow.

Compost is used to help make soil better and grow more nutritious vegetables. Katie has compost bins set up at home and at school. Do any of your friends or family use compost in their yards? Ask them about it.

garden supply stores, a grower's manual, and support from a master gardener are just a few. Gardens began to blossom in Massachusetts, Wisconsin, Georgia, and a few other states in 2009.

Not long after launching her nonprofit, the only soup kitchen in Katie's community shut down. She recognized that her gardens could offer a solution and started Katie's Krops Dinners. Once or twice a month, Katie and her volunteers serve meals prepared primarily with the

Many people volunteer at soup kitchens during the holidays. But these organizations need help year round.

19

harvest from their gardens to anyone in need.

   As of 2017, there were more than 100 gardens in 33 states. These gardens have fed thousands of people. Currently a college student, Katie remains very active in the charity she **cultivated**, while Stacy takes care of the charity's day-to-day needs. Katie returns home for the Katie's Krops Dinners, reviews grant proposals, and never misses a chance to garden locally.

Katie's favorite crop to grow is a cabbage. Her favorite to eat is eggplant. What is your favorite vegetable?

Grow something! Some vegetables can be grown in small pots indoors. Start your own kitchen garden with vegetable seeds and small jars or pots. What yummy veggies do you want to grow?

GLOSSARY

bounty (BOUN-tee) something, such as crops, that exists in generous amounts

cultivated (KUHL-tuh-vay-tid) promoted the growth and development of something

empowering (em-POU-ur-ing) helping someone believe they are powerful and can change things or go after their dreams

grants (GRANTS) sums of money to be used for a particular purpose

harvests (HAHR-vists) crops that have been gathered at the end of a growing season

maintenance (MAYN-tuh-nuhns) care and upkeep

philanthropist (fuh-LAN-thruh-pist) a person who works to promote the general welfare of others

resolved (rih-ZAHLVD) came to a definite decision

seedling (SEED-ling) a young plant grown from a seed

FIND OUT MORE

WEB SITES

www.katieskrops.com
Learn more about Katie, the crops she's produced, and how to start
your own Katie's Krop.

www.fruitsandveggiesmorematters.org
Fruits & Veggies: More Matters is a program that focuses on helping
Americans eat more fruits and vegetables for better health.

www.homelessshelterdirectory.org
Use this site to find homeless shelters, food pantries, and other ways
to get or give help.

INDEX

ABOUT THE AUTHOR

Melissa Sherman Pearl is a mother of two girls who understands and appreciates that you don't have to be an adult to make a difference.

24